A helping at meal

This book belongs to

_____

Written by Stephen Barnett
Illustrated by Rosie Brooks

Contents

A helping hand at mealtimes 3

New words 31

What did you learn? 32

About this book

This book makes young readers aware of good table manners. It throws light on family values as well. Along with this, this book helps children sharpen their language and vocabulary skills as well.

A helping hand at mealtimes

My family likes to eat their meals together.

I am David.

This is my sister Ellen.

It is time for our meal.

Ellen and I set the table.

Today a friend will eat with us.

We wash our hands before we eat.

We wait for everyone to get their plates.

We talk to everyone while eating.

Can I serve you some more?

When we finish eating, we ask our parents if we can leave the table.

Then we help to clear away the plates and push in the chairs.

We thank our mother for making the meal.

Then we go out to play!

New words

before	plate
chairs	sister
everyone	start
family	table
friend	today
hands	together
leave	until
likes	wait
meals	wash
parents	

What did you learn?

What is the name of David's sister?

Who puts the plates on the table?

How many children are there at the table?

What do the children do after dinner?